Scholastic Success With

GRAMMAR

WORKBOOK

GRADE 3

SCHOLASTIC
PROFESSIONAL BOOKS

**New York • Toronto • London • Auckland • Sydney • Mexico City
New Delhi • Hong Kong • Buenos Aires**

ABOUT THE BOOK

"Nothing Succeeds Like Success."
—Alexandre Dumas the Elder, 1854

And no other resource boosts kids' grammar skills like *Scholastic Success With Grammar*! For classroom or at-home use, this exciting series for kids in grades 1 through 6 provides invaluable reinforcement and practice in grammar topics such as:

- sentence types
- parts of speech
- common and proper nouns
- sentence structure
- contractions
- verb tenses
- subject-verb agreement
- punctuation
- capitalization
- and more!

Each 64-page book contains loads of clever practice pages to keep kids challenged and excited as they strengthen the grammar skills they need to read and write well.

You'll also find lots of assessment sheets that give kids realistic practice in taking standardized tests—and help you see their progress!

What makes Scholastic Success With Grammar so solid?
Each practice page in the series reinforces a specific, age-appropriate skill as outlined in one or more of the following standardized tests:

- Iowa Tests of Basic Skills
- California Tests of Basic Skills
- California Achievement Test
- Metropolitan Achievement Test
- Stanford Achievement Test

Take the lead and help kids succeed with *Scholastic Success With Grammar*. Parents and teachers agree: No one helps kids succeed like Scholastic.

TABLE OF CONTENTS

ISBN: 0-439-43400-9

STATEMENTS AND QUESTIONS

> A **statement** is a sentence that tells something. It ends with a period. A **question** is a sentence that asks something. It ends with a question mark.

A. Read each sentence. Write _Q_ on the line if the sentence is a question. Write _S_ if the sentence is a statement.

1. Where did the ant live? _____

2. The ant had many cousins. _____

3. She found the crumb under a leaf. _____

4. How will she carry it? _____

5. Who came along first? _____

6. The lizard wouldn't help. _____

7. He said he was too cold. _____

8. Why did the rooster fly away? _____

B. The sentences below do not make sense. Rewrite the words in the correct order.

1. How crumb did carry the ant the?

_____

_____

2. She herself it carried.

_____

_____

STATEMENTS AND QUESTIONS

A **statement** begins with a capital letter and ends with a period. A **question** begins with a capital letter and ends with a question mark.

A. Rewrite each sentence correctly.
Begin each sentence with a capital letter.
Use periods and question marks correctly.

1. can we take a taxi downtown

_____

2. where does the bus go

_____

3. the people on the bus waved to us

_____

4. we got on the elevator

_____

5. should I push the elevator button

_____

B. Write a question. Then write an answer that is a statement.

1. Question: _____

_____

2. Statement: _____

_____

STATEMENTS AND QUESTIONS

Look at the underlined part of each sentence. Decide if it is correct. Fill in the bubble next to the correct answer.

1. The ant found a big crumb.
   - ⬭ Found the ant
   - ⬭ Ant the found
   - ⬭ correct as is

2. The ant needs help?
   - ⬭ help
   - ⬭ help.
   - ⬭ correct as is

3. The coyote not help would.
   - ⬭ help not would
   - ⬭ would not help
   - ⬭ correct as is

4. the ants live in an anthill.
   - ⬭ The ants
   - ⬭ the Ants
   - ⬭ correct as is

5. She has many cousins?
   - ⬭ cousins
   - ⬭ cousins.
   - ⬭ correct as is

6. the man didn't see the ant.
   - ⬭ The Man
   - ⬭ The man
   - ⬭ correct as is

7. Did he lose his hat?
   - ⬭ hat
   - ⬭ hat.
   - ⬭ correct as is

8. He ran the ant from.
   - ⬭ from the ant.
   - ⬭ ant from the.
   - ⬭ correct as is

9. I am the strongest?
   - ⬭ strongest.
   - ⬭ strongest
   - ⬭ correct as is

10. do you think you can?
   - ⬭ Do you
   - ⬭ Do You
   - ⬭ correct as is

EXCLAMATIONS AND COMMANDS

An **exclamation** is a sentence that shows strong feeling. It ends with an exclamation point. A **command** is a sentence that gives an order. It ends with a period.

A. Read each sentence. Write *E* on the line if the sentence is an exclamation. Write *C* if the sentence is a command.

1. They chase buffaloes! _____

2. You have to go, too. _____

3. Wait at the airport. _____

4. It snows all the time! _____

5. Alligators live in the sewers! _____

6. Look at the horse. _____

7. That's a great-looking horse! _____

8. Write a letter to Seymour. _____

B. Complete each exclamation and command. The punctuation mark at the end of each line is a clue.

1. I feel _____!

2. Help your _____.

3. That's a _____!

4. I lost _____!

5. Turn the _____.

6. Come watch the _____.

7. Please let me _____.

EXCLAMATIONS AND COMMANDS

> A **sentence** tells a complete thought. It tells who or what, and it tells what happens.

A. Draw a line between the words in Column A and Column B to form complete sentences. Then write the complete sentences on the lines below. Remember to add an exclamation mark or a period.

Column A	Column B
There's a	the buffaloes
Look at	your toys and games
Pack	Gila monster at the airport

1. _____

2. _____

3. _____

B. Write *sentence* after each complete thought. Write *not a sentence* after each incomplete thought. Then make each incomplete thought into a sentence.

1. I ate a salami sandwich. _____

2. I like to ride horses. _____

3. Subway driver. _____

4. There are horned toads. _____

5. Kids on our street _____

6. We are moving tomorrow. _____

EXCLAMATIONS AND COMMANDS

Look at the underlined part of each sentence. Decide if it is correct. Fill in the bubble next to the correct answer.

1. I'm going to Texas!
   - ◯ I'm going to Texas?
   - ◯ I'm to Texas!
   - ◯ correct as is

2. I am so excited
   - ◯ excited!
   - ◯ excited?
   - ◯ correct as is

3. Please help me pack
   - ◯ pack?
   - ◯ pack.
   - ◯ correct as is

4. Her baby brother is adorable
   - ◯ adorable?
   - ◯ adorable!
   - ◯ correct as is

5. I can't wait!
   - ◯ wait.
   - ◯ wait
   - ◯ correct as is

6. Help me find.
   - ◯ Help me find a game.
   - ◯ Help find game.
   - ◯ correct as is

7. We'll have such fun!
   - ◯ fun
   - ◯ fun?
   - ◯ correct as is

8. It be!
   - ◯ It will be great!
   - ◯ It great!
   - ◯ correct as is

9. Remember to write to me
   - ◯ to write to
   - ◯ to write to me.
   - ◯ correct as is

10. My team the game!
    - ◯ team won the game!
    - ◯ team won game!
    - ◯ correct as is

Name

SINGULAR AND PLURAL NOUNS

A **singular noun** names one person, place, or thing. A **plural noun** names more than one person, place, or thing. Add -s to form the plural of most nouns.

A. Each sentence has an underlined noun.
   On the line, write *S* if it is a singular noun.
   Write *P* if it is a plural noun.

1. She has a new baby. _____

2. It is very cute. _____

3. She has small fingers. _____

4. She drinks from a bottle. _____

5. I can tell my friends all about it. _____

B. Read each sentence. Underline the singular noun.
   Circle the plural noun.

1. The baby has two sisters.

2. The nightgown has pockets.

3. Her hand has tiny fingers.

4. My parents have a baby.

5. The family has three girls.

C. Complete the chart. Write the singular or plural of each noun.

Singular	Plural
fence	
	trains
gate	
	cows

Name _____

SINGULAR AND PLURAL NOUNS

A singular noun names one person, place, or thing. A plural noun names more than one person, place, or thing. Add -s to form the plural of most nouns. Add -es to form the plural of nouns that end in ss, x, ch, or sh. Some nouns change their spelling to form the plural.

A. Finish the chart. Write singular nouns in each column.

Nouns that end in *ch, sh, ss, x*	Nouns that end in *y*	Nouns that end in *f*
bench	party	loaf

B. Complete each sentence with the plural form of the noun in ( ).

1. Mia picks _____ from the trees in her backyard. (cherry)

2. There are also many _____ with tiny berries. (bush)

3. Fresh _____ are her favorite snack. (peach)

4. She loads _____ with these different fruits. (box)

5. The kitchen _____ are filled with delicious jams. (shelf)

6. Mia shares the fruit with the third-grade _____. (class)

C. Use the words *story* and *stories* in one sentence. Use *fox* and *foxes* in another sentence.

1. _____

_____

2. _____

_____

Scholastic Success With Grammar • Grade 3 **11**

SINGULAR AND PLURAL NOUNS

**Read each riddle. Decide if the underlined noun is correct.
Fill in the bubble next to the correct answer.**

1. We are square and made from
   cardboard. We are <u>boxs</u>.

   ⬭ boxes
   ⬭ box
   ⬭ correct as is

2. We help you chew your food.
   We are <u>tooth</u>.

   ⬭ tooths
   ⬭ teeth
   ⬭ correct as is

3. You can find us on a farm.
   We are <u>geese</u>.

   ⬭ goose
   ⬭ gooses
   ⬭ correct as is

4. Be sure not to drop us when you
   take a drink. We are <u>glassess</u>.

   ⬭ glass
   ⬭ glasses
   ⬭ correct as is

5. We are messages sent over
   telephone lines. We are <u>fax</u>.

   ⬭ faxs
   ⬭ faxes
   ⬭ correct as is

6. You can use us to comb your hair.
   We are <u>brush.</u>

   ⬭ brushes
   ⬭ brushs
   ⬭ correct as is

7. You can buy us in a food store.
   We are <u>grocerys</u>.

   ⬭ grocery
   ⬭ groceries
   ⬭ correct as is

8. We are places trains can stop.
   We are <u>stations</u>.

   ⬭ station
   ⬭ stationes
   ⬭ correct as is

9. We like to eat cheese.
   We are <u>mouse</u>.

   ⬭ mice
   ⬭ mices
   ⬭ correct as is

10. We are tales to read. We are <u>story</u>.

    ⬭ stories
    ⬭ storys
    ⬭ correct as is

Name _____

COMMON AND PROPER NOUNS

A **common noun** names any person, place, or thing. A **proper noun** names a particular person, place, or thing. A proper noun begins with a capital letter.

A. Is the underlined word a common noun or a proper noun? Write *common* or *proper*.

1. The <u>girl</u> likes to learn. _____

2. She goes to two <u>schools</u>. _____

3. She lives in <u>America</u>. _____

B. Underline the common nouns. Circle the proper nouns.

1. April has a brother and a sister.

2. Their names are Julius and May.

3. Their parents were born in Taiwan.

4. April goes to school on Saturday.

5. She is learning a language called Mandarin.

6. May read a book about the Middle Ages.

C. Underline the common nouns. Circle the proper nouns. Then write them on the chart in the correct category.

1. Last August David went to camp.

2. Many children go to a picnic on the Fourth of July.

Common Nouns	Proper Nouns
_____	_____
_____	_____
_____	_____

Name

COMMON AND PROPER NOUNS

A **common noun** names any person, place, or thing. A **proper noun** names a particular person, place, or thing. A proper noun begins with a capital letter.

A. Read each word in the box.
Write it where it belongs on the chart.

doctor   park   football   Tangram   Pat   Atlanta

Category	Common Nouns	Proper Nouns
1. Person		
2. Place		
3. Thing		

B. Complete each sentence with a common noun or proper noun. In the box, write *C* if you wrote a common noun. Write *P* if you wrote a proper noun.

1. I threw the ball to _____. (person) ☐

2. I have visited _____. (place) ☐

3. My favorite food is _____. (thing) ☐

4. My family lives in _____. (place) ☐

5. My favorite author is _____. (person) ☐

6. I wish I had a _____. (thing) ☐

7. I like to read about _____. (historical event) ☐

8. My favorite holiday is _____. (holiday) ☐

Name _____

ASSESSMENT

COMMON AND PROPER NOUNS

Is the underlined part of each sentence correct? Fill in the bubble next to the right answer.

1. The fourth of July is my favorite holiday.
   - ◯ Fourth of July
   - ◯ fourth of july
   - ◯ correct as is

2. In Australia, winter begins in the month of June.
   - ◯ Month of June
   - ◯ month of june
   - ◯ correct as is

3. I love tom's apple pie.
   - ◯ Tom's apple pie
   - ◯ tom's Apple Pie
   - ◯ correct as is

4. Our teacher, Dr. ruffin, is from Louisiana.
   - ◯ teacher, dr. Ruffin
   - ◯ teacher, Dr. Ruffin
   - ◯ correct as is

5. He speaks Spanish and Japanese.
   - ◯ spanish and japanese
   - ◯ Spanish and japanese
   - ◯ correct as is

6. Susan's family is from Kansas City, missouri.
   - ◯ Kansas City, Missouri
   - ◯ kansas city, Missouri
   - ◯ correct as is

7. Let's have a new year's day party!
   - ◯ new year's Day
   - ◯ New Year's Day
   - ◯ correct as is

8. There will be no school on monday.
   - ◯ School on Monday
   - ◯ school on Monday
   - ◯ correct as is

9. Dogs are the most popular pets in north america.
   - ◯ pets in North America
   - ◯ pets in North america
   - ◯ correct as is

10. Do you want to go to the Movies on Saturday?
    - ◯ the movies on Saturday
    - ◯ the Movies on saturday
    - ◯ correct as is

SINGULAR AND PLURAL PRONOUNS

> A **singular pronoun** takes the place of a noun that names one person, place, or thing.
> A **plural pronoun** takes the place of a noun that names more than one person, place, or thing.

**A. Underline the pronoun in each sentence.
On the line, write *S* if it is singular or *P* if it is plural.**

1. He is called Spider. _____

2. I can see Spider has eight long legs. _____

3. They asked Spider a question. _____

4. We want to know what's in the pot. _____

5. It contains all the wisdom in the world. _____

**B. Read each pair of sentences. Circle the pronoun in the second
sentence. Then underline the word or words in the first sentence
that it replaces. Write the pronoun under *Singular* or *Plural*.**

	Singular	Plural
1. This story is funny. It is about wisdom.	_____	_____
2. The author retold the story. She is a good writer.	_____	_____
3. My friends and I read the story aloud. We enjoyed the ending.	_____	_____
4. Two boys acted out a scene. They each took a different role.	_____	_____

C. For each noun write a subject pronoun that could take its place.

1. Spider _____   3. Tortoise and Hare _____

2. the pot _____   4. Spider's mother _____

SINGULAR AND PLURAL PRONOUNS

> A **subject pronoun** takes the place of a noun or nouns as the subject of a sentence. A subject pronoun can be singular or plural. *I, you, she, he, it, we,* and *they* are subject pronouns. An **object pronoun** takes the place of a noun or nouns in the predicate. An **object pronoun** can be singular or plural. *Me, you, him, her, it, us,* and *them* are object pronouns.

A. Underline the object pronoun in each sentence. Circle *S* if it is singular or *P* if it is plural.

1. Darren and Tracy were playing soccer with us.　　　S or P

2. Tracy passed the ball to him.　　　S or P

3. He kicked the ball back to her.　　　S or P

4. She stopped it in front of the net.　　　S or P

5. Tracy kicked the ball toward me.　　　S or P

6. I kept them from scoring a goal.　　　S or P

B. Complete each sentence. Write the correct pronoun in ( ) on the line.

1. Ms. Stone gave _____ a funny assignment. (we, us)

2. She asked _____ to tell a funny story. (I, me)

3. Ray and Pete brought _____ a book of jokes. (she, her)

4. She thanked _____. (them, they)

5. Dina acted out a story with _____. (him, he)

C. Write one sentence using *it* as a subject pronoun.
   Write another sentence using *it* as an object pronoun.

_____

_____

SINGULAR AND PLURAL PRONOUNS

Is the underlined pronoun correct? Fill in the bubble next to the right answer.

1. My parents took the three of we to a garage sale.
   - ○ us
   - ○ her
   - ○ I
   - ○ correct as is

2. Mom and Dad really wanted I to go.
   - ○ She
   - ○ They
   - ○ me
   - ○ correct as is

3. Mom wouldn't take "no" for an answer. She said that I might find something good.
   - ○ Her
   - ○ Them
   - ○ Me
   - ○ correct as is

4. The drive was boring. He was the longest trip I'd ever taken.
   - ○ She
   - ○ They
   - ○ It
   - ○ correct as is

5. My two sisters were sleepy. I let they lean on me.
   - ○ them
   - ○ us
   - ○ she
   - ○ correct as is

6. Dad found some golf clubs. Him was so excited.
   - ○ You
   - ○ He
   - ○ Me
   - ○ correct as is

7. Mom liked a vase. Dad bought it for her.
   - ○ she
   - ○ I
   - ○ they
   - ○ correct as is

8. Sonya and Kara both found mysteries. They began to read right away.
   - ○ Her
   - ○ It
   - ○ Them
   - ○ correct as is

9. There was a dusty box in the corner. Him was covered in cobwebs.
   - ○ Them
   - ○ Her
   - ○ It
   - ○ correct as is

10. I pulled out an old baseball mitt. Me was so surprised!
    - ○ I
    - ○ Him
    - ○ Them
    - ○ correct as is

ACTION VERBS

A. Underline the action verb in each sentence.

1. The villagers cheered loudly.

2. They added flavor to the cheese.

3. Please give them the milk.

4. He serves the cheese.

5. He emptied the buckets.

B. Circle the action verb in ( ) that paints a more vivid picture of what the subject is doing.

1. The villagers (walked, paraded) across the floor.

2. Father (whispered, talked) to the baby.

3. The puppy (ate, gobbled) down his food.

4. The girl (skipped, went) to her chair.

5. The ball (fell, bounced) down the stairs.

C. Write an action verb from the box to complete each sentence.

whispered   laughed   sighed

1. We _____ at the playful kittens.

2. She _____ deeply and fell asleep.

3. Megan _____ to her friend in the library.

ACTION VERBS

A. On the line, write the action verb in ( ) that paints a clearer picture.

1. A squirrel _____ an acorn. (took, snatched)

2. It _____ the acorn open. (cracked, broke)

3. The squirrel _____ the nut. (nibbled, ate)

4. Then it _____ up the tree. (went, scrambled)

B. Circle each verb. Then write the verb from the box that gives a livelier picture of the action.

| shouted | honked | ran | bounced | grabbed |

1. The bus driver blew the horn.   _____

2. The girl got her books.   _____

3. She said, "Good-bye," to her family.   _____

4. She went to the bus.   _____

5. The bus moved down the bumpy road.   _____

C. Write two sentences that show action. Use the verb *dashed* in the first sentence. Use the word *tiptoed* in the second sentence. Underline the verbs.

1. _____

2. _____

Name

ACTION VERBS

A. Fill in the bubble next to the action verb in each sentence.

1. Crystal's whole family arrived for dinner.
   - ○ dinner
   - ○ family
   - ○ arrived

2. Her grandmother hugged everyone.
   - ○ grandmother
   - ○ hugged
   - ○ everyone

3. Her aunt and uncle roasted a huge turkey.
   - ○ roasted
   - ○ turkey
   - ○ huge

4. Everyone ate the delicious meal.
   - ○ ate
   - ○ Everyone
   - ○ meal

5. They cheered for the cooks!
   - ○ cooks
   - ○ They
   - ○ cheered

B. Read each sentence. Fill in the bubble next to the more vivid verb.

1. The puppy _____ after the ball.
   - ○ went
   - ○ chased

2. She _____ all around the house and yard.
   - ○ dashed
   - ○ went

3. A yellow cat _____ through the wooden fence.
   - ○ looked
   - ○ peeked

4. Then the puppy _____ high into the air.
   - ○ leaped
   - ○ moved

5. She _____ the ball.
   - ○ got
   - ○ grabbed

PRESENT- AND PAST-TENSE VERBS

> **Present-tense verbs** show action that is happening now. They agree in number with who or what is doing the action. **Past-tense verbs** show action that took place in the past. Most past-tense verbs end in *-ed*.

A. Read each sentence. If the underlined verb is in the present tense, write *present* on the line. If it is in the past tense, write *past*.

1. We worked together on a jigsaw puzzle. _____

2. Mom helped us. _____

3. She enjoys puzzles, too. _____

4. Tom picked out the border pieces. _____

5. He dropped a puzzle piece on the floor. _____

6. I looked for the flower pieces. _____

7. Dad likes crossword puzzles better. _____

8. My little sister watches us. _____

9. Mom hurries us before dinner. _____

10. We rushed to finish quickly. _____

B. Underline the verb in each sentence. Then rewrite the sentence. Change the present-tense verb to the past. Change the past-tense verb to the present.

1. The man crosses the river.

_____

2. He rowed his boat.

_____

PRESENT- AND PAST-TENSE VERBS

> **Present-tense verbs** must agree in number with the subject. The letters -s or -es are usually added to a present-tense verb when the subject of the sentence is a singular noun or *he, she,* or *it.*

A. Read each sentence. On the line, write the correct form of the present-tense verb in ( ).

1. The crow _____ the pitcher with pebbles. (fill, fills)

2. The man _____ the crow. (watch, watches)

3. Then he _____ the cabbage across the river. (take, takes)

4. The man and the goat _____ the wolf behind. (leave, leaves)

5. They _____ back on the last trip. (go, goes)

B. Write the correct past-tense form of the verb in ( ).

1. J.J. _____ for the hidden picture. (look)

2. He _____ at it for a long time. (stare)

3. Ana _____ by. (walk)

4. Then she _____ solve the puzzle. (help)

C. Write three sentences. Use the verb in ( ) in your sentence.

1. (play) _____

   _____

2. (plays)_____

   _____

3. (played) _____

   _____

PRESENT- AND PAST-TENSE VERBS

Is the underlined verb in each sentence correct? Fill in the
bubble next to the right answer.

1. Mr. Henry bakes delicious apple
pies.

- ◯ bake
- ◯ baking
- ◯ correct as is

2. He wash and peel each apple
carefully.

- ◯ washes and peels
- ◯ wash and peeled
- ◯ correct as is

3. He slices each apple into eight
pieces.

- ◯ slicing
- ◯ slice
- ◯ correct as is

4. Mr. Henry's children enjoys the pies
very much.

- ◯ enjoy
- ◯ enjoying
- ◯ correct as is

5. Last summer, Mr. Henry enter a
pie-baking contest.

- ◯ enters
- ◯ entered
- ◯ correct as is

6. His whole family travel to the
competition.

- ◯ traveling
- ◯ traveled
- ◯ correct as is

7. They arrives just in time.

- ◯ arriving
- ◯ arrived
- ◯ correct as is

8. The judges awards Mr. Henry's pie
a blue ribbon.

- ◯ awarded
- ◯ awarding
- ◯ correct as is

9. They tasted Mr. Henry's pie and
said it was wonderful.

- ◯ tastes
- ◯ taste
- ◯ correct as is

10. All the people enjoys the day!

- ◯ enjoying
- ◯ enjoyed
- ◯ correct as is

THE VERB *BE*

> The verb **be** tells what the subject of a sentence is or was. *Am, is,* and *are* tell about someone or something in the present. *Was* and *were* tell about someone or something in the past.

A. **Read each sentence. Circle the word that is a form of the verb *be*.**

1. Captain Fossy was Mr. Anning's good friend.

2. Mary Anning said, "The dragon is gigantic!"

3. "Its eyes are as big as saucers!" she told her mother.

4. "I am inside the cave!" she shouted to her brother.

5. The scientists were amazed by the remarkable fossil.

B. **Read each sentence. If the underlined verb is in the past tense, write *past* on the line. If it is in the present tense, write *present*.**

1. Mary Anning was a real person. _____

2. I am interested in fossils, too. _____

3. There are many dinosaurs in the museum. _____

4. The exhibits were closed yesterday. _____

5. This is a map of the first floor. _____

C. **Write the form of *be* that completes each sentence.**

am   is   are

1. I _____ on the bus with my mother and father.

2. Buses _____ fun to ride.

3. The bus driver _____ a friendly woman.

Name _____

THE VERB *BE*

> Some verbs show action. Others, such as the verb **be**, show being, or what something is or was. The form of be must agree with the subject of the sentence.

A. Circle each verb. If the verb shows action, write *action* on the line. If the verb shows being, write *being*.

1. The sunshine is bright and hot. _____

2. We carried our umbrellas. _____

3. The sailboats were still. _____

4. There are no rocks on the beach. _____

B. Circle the verb that best completes the sentence. Remember that the form of the verb *be* must agree with the subject.

1. I (is, am) a third grader.

2. Pat and I (is, are) partners in class.

3. Jimmy (was, were) my partner last month.

4. Mrs. Boynton (is, are) the science teacher.

5. The students (was, were) interested in the experiment.

C. Write two sentences that tell about someone or something. Use *is* in one sentence. Use *was* in the other.

1. _____

_____

2. _____

_____

THE VERB *BE*

Is the underlined verb in each sentence correct? Fill in the bubble next to the right answer.

1. All dinosaurs <u>is</u> extinct.
   - ○ am
   - ○ are
   - ○ correct as is

2. A brontosaurus <u>is</u> a kind of dinosaur.
   - ○ am
   - ○ are
   - ○ correct as is

3. Many people <u>are</u> puzzled about what happened to dinosaurs.
   - ○ am
   - ○ was
   - ○ correct as is

4. Dinosaurs <u>was</u> plant-eaters or meat-eaters.
   - ○ is
   - ○ were
   - ○ correct as is

5. I <u>are</u> interested in Tyrannosaurus rex.
   - ○ am
   - ○ were
   - ○ correct as is

6. It <u>were</u> a fierce meat-eater.
   - ○ are
   - ○ was
   - ○ correct as is

7. Dinosaurs <u>was</u> like some reptiles that live today.
   - ○ is
   - ○ were
   - ○ correct as is

8. Their teeth, bones, and skin <u>was</u> like those of crocodiles.
   - ○ were
   - ○ is
   - ○ correct as is

9. Large dinosaurs <u>were</u> the largest land animals that ever lived.
   - ○ am
   - ○ was
   - ○ correct as is

10. I <u>are</u> amazed by their extraordinary size!
    - ○ am
    - ○ were
    - ○ correct as is

MAIN VERBS AND HELPING VERBS

> A **main verb** is the most important verb in a sentence. It shows the action. A **helping verb** works with the main verb. Forms of *be* and *have* are helping verbs. The helping verb *will* shows future tense.

A. Read each sentence. Write *M* if a main verb is underlined. Write *H* if a helping verb is underlined. Circle the main and helping verbs that show future tense.

1. We will learn about new buildings. _____

2. The backhoe is digging the foundation. _____

3. It had filled several dump trucks. _____

4. The dump trucks are removing the dirt. _____

5. Workers are building the outer wall. _____

6. A cement truck is pouring the concrete. _____

7. It will need several days to dry. _____

8. At noon the workers will eat their lunch. _____

B. Choose the correct main and helping verb from the box to complete each sentence. Write it on the line. Circle the main and helping verbs that show future tense.

had climbed	have lifted	will watch	are reading	is going

1. We _____ a movie about skyscrapers.

2. A building _____ up.

3. The workers _____ the plans.

4. Cranes _____ the heavy beams.

5. A worker _____ a tall ladder.

MAIN VERBS AND HELPING VERBS

> A **main verb** is the most important verb in a sentence. It shows the action. A **helping verb** works with the main verb. Forms of *be* and *have* are helping verbs.

A. Read each sentence. Circle the helping verb. Draw a line under the main verb.

1. Jamal had built his first model rocket last year.

2. He has painted it red, white, and blue.

3. Now Jamal is building another rocket.

4. It will fly many feet into the air.

5. A parachute will bring the rocket back to Jamal.

6. I am buying a model rocket, too.

B. Complete each sentence with the correct main verb or helping verb in ( ). Write the word on the line.

1. Kim _____ making a clay vase. (is, has)

2. The clay _____ arrived yesterday. (was, had)

3. I am _____ to watch her work. (go, going)

4. She is _____ a potter's wheel. (used, using)

5. The sculpture _____ go above the fireplace. (will, is)

6. People _____ admired Kim's beautiful vases. (are, have)

C. Write two sentences about something you will do later in the week. Use the future tense helping verb. Be sure to use a main verb and helping verb in each sentence.

1. _____

2. _____

MAIN VERBS AND HELPING VERBS

A. Read each sentence. Fill in the bubble next to the main verb.

1. Ed is reading a book in the park.
   - ◯ Ed
   - ◯ is
   - ◯ reading

2. The children are playing baseball nearby.
   - ◯ are
   - ◯ playing
   - ◯ baseball

3. I have walked to the park, too.
   - ◯ walked
   - ◯ have
   - ◯ park

4. Tomorrow, my sister will come along.
   - ◯ Tomorrow
   - ◯ come
   - ◯ will

5. She will share her lunch with me.
   - ◯ share
   - ◯ will
   - ◯ lunch

B. Read each sentence. Fill in the bubble next to the helping verb.

1. Jill has visited her grandparents many times this year.
   - ◯ Jill
   - ◯ has
   - ◯ visited

2. She is sending them an E-mail now.
   - ◯ E-mail
   - ◯ is
   - ◯ sending

3. In June, they will drive to Washington, D.C.
   - ◯ they
   - ◯ driving
   - ◯ will

4. Jill and her brother will go with them.
   - ◯ will
   - ◯ go
   - ◯ them

5. They have waited for this trip for a long time.
   - ◯ waited
   - ◯ this
   - ◯ have

LINKING VERBS

> A **linking verb** tells what someone or something is, was, or will be. The linking verb most often used is a form of the verb *be*, such as *am, is, are, was, were,* and *will be.*

A. Find the linking verb in each sentence. Write it on the line.

1. This book is a biography about Thomas Edison. _____

2. I am interested in books about inventors. _____

3. Thomas Edison was a hard worker. _____

4. His inventions were wonderful. _____

5. They are still important for us today. _____

6. You will be amazed by this book. _____

B. Read each sentence and underline the linking verb. Then circle the word that tells if it is past or present.

1. I am a fan of Thomas Edison.   Past or Present

2. Thomas Edison was a famous inventor.   Past or Present

3. Many of his inventions are well-known.   Past or Present

4. His parents were friendly.   Past or Present

5. Jared is Edison's great-great-grandson.   Past or Present

C. Finish each sentence correctly. Write *are, am,* or *was* on the line.

1. I _____ excited.

2. This book _____ great!

3. Inventors _____ interesting people.

LINKING VERBS

> A **linking verb** tells what someone or something is, was, or will be. *Am, is,* and *was* are used when the subject of the sentence is singular. *Are* and *were* are used when the subject is plural. *Are* and *were* are also used with *you.*

A. Underline the linking verb in each sentence. Circle *S* if the subject is singular. Circle *P* if the subject is plural.

1. I was very bored.   S or P

2. Now I am so happy.   S or P

3. Stacey and Leda are my new neighbors.   S or P

4. They were surprised by my visit.   S or P

5. Stacey is very funny.   S or P

B. Complete each sentence with the correct linking verb in ( ). Write the word on the line.

1. Roberto Clemente _____ a great baseball player. (was, were)

2. All baseball fans _____ amazed by his talents. (were, was)

3. I _____ one of his biggest fans. (is, am)

4. He _____ a true hero to me. (are, is)

5. Sammy Sosa and Henry Aaron _____ my other favorite players. (is, are)

C. Think of a favorite animal. Write two sentences to describe it. Use one of these linking verbs in each sentence: *am, is, are, was, were, will be.*

_____

_____

LINKING VERBS

A. Read each sentence. Fill in the bubble next to the linking verb.

1. My new computer is fast.
   - ○ new
   - ○ is
   - ○ fast

2. I am excited about it.
   - ○ am
   - ○ I
   - ○ excited

3. The two mouse pads are colorful.
   - ○ two
   - ○ pads
   - ○ are

4. The speakers were heavy.
   - ○ were
   - ○ heavy
   - ○ speakers

5. All of the software was free.
   - ○ software
   - ○ was
   - ○ free

B. Read each sentence. Fill in the bubble next to the correct linking verb.

1. My mom _____ a rafting teacher.
   - ○ is
   - ○ are
   - ○ were

2. The trip last week _____ so much fun.
   - ○ will be
   - ○ were
   - ○ was

3. The rafts _____ very soft and bouncy.
   - ○ are
   - ○ is
   - ○ was

4. Yesterday, the docks _____ crowded.
   - ○ will be
   - ○ was
   - ○ were

5. I _____ a raft instructor in the future.
   - ○ will be
   - ○ am
   - ○ is

SUBJECTS AND PREDICATES

A. Draw a line between the complete subject and the complete predicate.

> The **complete subject** tells whom or what the sentence is about. The **complete predicate** tells who or what the subject is or does. The **simple subject** is the main word in the complete subject. The **simple predicate** is the verb in the complete predicate.

1. All of the families traveled to California.

2. Baby Betsy, Billy, Joe, and Ted stayed in the cabin.

3. My father told us stories.

4. I baked a pie.

B. Draw a circle around the simple subject in each sentence. Then write it on the line.

1. Betsy learned how to walk. _____

2. The miners ate it up. _____

3. The new baby looks like me. _____

4. My feet are tired. _____

5. The man started a laundry. _____

C. Draw a circle around the simple predicate in each sentence. Then write it on the line.

1. We made a pie together. _____

2. First we rolled the crust. _____

3. Then we added the berries. _____

4. It bakes for one hour. _____

5. Everybody loves our pie! _____

SUBJECTS AND PREDICATES

> The **simple subject** is the main word in the complete subject. The **simple predicate** is the main word in the complete predicate.

A. Read each sentence. Draw a line between the complete subject and the complete predicate. Then write the simple subject and the simple predicate.

	Simple Subject	Simple Predicate
1. Mrs. Perez's class took a trip to the museum.	_____	_____
2. Many large paintings hung on the walls.	_____	_____
3. Maria saw a painting of an animal alphabet.	_____	_____
4. All the children looked at the painting.	_____	_____
5. Paul pointed to a cat on a leash.	_____	_____
6. His friend liked the dancing zebra.	_____	_____
7. Everyone laughed at the purple cow.	_____	_____
8. Many people visited the museum that day.	_____	_____
9. The bus took us to school.	_____	_____

B. Finish the sentences. Add a complete subject to sentence 1. Add a complete predicate to sentence 2.

1. _____ was funny.

2. My class _____.

SUBJECTS AND PREDICATES

A. Is the underlined part of the sentence the complete subject or a complete predicate? Fill in the bubble next to the correct answer.

1. My little brother carried his backpack.
   - ○ complete subject
   - ○ complete predicate

2. I found my old fishing rod.
   - ○ complete subject
   - ○ complete predicate

3. My dad put air in our bicycle tires.
   - ○ complete subject
   - ○ complete predicate

4. Our whole family rode to the big lake.
   - ○ complete subject
   - ○ complete predicate

5. Many pink flowers bloomed on the trees.
   - ○ complete subject
   - ○ complete predicate

B. Fill in the bubble that tells if the underlined word is the simple subject or the simple predicate.

1. A man rowed a boat on the lake.
   - ○ simple subject
   - ○ simple predicate

2. My brother played ball in the field.
   - ○ simple subject
   - ○ simple predicate

3. Some other children joined in the game.
   - ○ simple subject
   - ○ simple predicate

4. Our large basket sat unopened on the picnic table.
   - ○ simple subject
   - ○ simple predicate

5. We ate cheese sandwiches and fruit.
   - ○ simple subject
   - ○ simple predicate

ADJECTIVES

> **Adjectives** describe nouns. They can tell what color, size, and shape something is. They can also tell how something sounds, feels, or tastes.

A. Look at each underlined noun. Circle the adjective or adjectives that describe it. Then write the adjectives on the lines.

1. My big <u>brother</u> likes to eat sweet <u>fruits</u>.   _____   _____

2. He eats them on many hot <u>days</u>.   _____   _____

3. He cuts the red <u>apple</u> into four <u>pieces</u>.   _____   _____

4. The ripe <u>bananas</u> and juicy peaches are his favorites.   _____   _____

5. Mom bought him a large, round <u>watermelon</u>.   _____   _____

6. He made a delicious, colorful <u>salad</u> for all of us!   _____   _____

B. Write two adjectives to describe each noun. Use words that describe color, size, shape, sound, or how something tastes or feels.

1. the _____, _____ balloon

2. a _____, _____ apple

3. a _____, _____ day

C. Write a sentence about a pet. Use two adjectives to describe the pet.

_____

_____

ADJECTIVES

> An **adjective** is a word that describes a person, place, or thing.

A. Read each sentence. Write the adjective that describes the underlined noun on the line.

1. We live near a sparkling <u>brook</u>. _____

2. It has clear <u>water</u>. _____

3. Large <u>fish</u> swim in the brook. _____

4. Busy <u>squirrels</u> play near the brook. _____

5. You can enjoy breathing in the fresh <u>air</u> near the brook. _____

B. Complete each sentence by adding an adjective.

1. I love _____ apples.

2. I see a _____ ball.

3. I smell _____ flowers.

4. I hear _____ music.

5. I like the _____ taste of pickles.

Write three sentences that tell about the foods you like the best. Use adjectives in your description.

ADJECTIVES

A. Read each sentence. Fill in the bubble next to the word that is an adjective.

1. Several relatives from Mexico visited us.
   - ○ Several
   - ○ relatives
   - ○ visited

2. The trip took six hours.
   - ○ trip
   - ○ six
   - ○ hours

3. They took many pictures of my family.
   - ○ took
   - ○ many
   - ○ pictures

4. My uncle wore a blue hat.
   - ○ uncle
   - ○ blue
   - ○ hat

5. My aunt wore a colorful *serape*.
   - ○ aunt
   - ○ wore
   - ○ colorful

B. Fill in the bubble next to the adjective that best completes the sentence.

1. We ate the _____ food.
   - ○ loud
   - ○ fuzzy
   - ○ delicious

2. There were _____ people in the restaurant.
   - ○ one
   - ○ many
   - ○ green

3. My dad ordered _____ tortillas.
   - ○ sharp
   - ○ loud
   - ○ some

4. My cousin José ate _____ tamales!
   - ○ noisy
   - ○ five
   - ○ curly

5. Everyone had a _____ time!
   - ○ cold
   - ○ wonderful
   - ○ purple

ARTICLES AND OTHER ADJECTIVES

The words *a*, *an*, and *the* are special adjectives called **articles**. **A** is used before words that begin with a consonant. **An** is used before words that begin with a vowel. **The** is used before either.

A. Circle the articles in each sentence.

1. The elk, moose, and bears grazed in the forest.

2. There was an abundant supply of grass and plants.

3. A bolt of lightning struck a tree and started a fire.

4. Fires have always been an important part of forest ecology.

5. The heat of the summer left the forest very dry.

6. The fires spread over a thousand acres.

7. The helicopters and an airplane spread chemicals on the fire.

8. Firefighters made an attempt to stop the flames.

B. Circle the article in ( ) that completes each sentence correctly. Then write it on the line.

1. Last summer I visited _____ National Park. (a, an)

2. We took a bus through _____ forests. (an, the)

3. The bus carried us up _____ narrow roads. (a, the)

4. I saw _____ elk grazing on some grass. (a, an)

5. We stayed in _____ old log cabin. (a, an)

6. Deer came up to _____ cabin window. (an, the)

7. We made _____ new friend. (a, an)

8. I wrote my friend _____ letter. (a, an)

Articles and Other Adjectives

The article **A** is used before words that begin with a consonant. **An** is used before words that begin with a vowel. **The** is used efore either.

A. Circle the article that correctly completes the sentence.

1. I saw (a, an) octopus at the aquarium.

2. A trainer was feeding fish to (a, an) dolphin.

3. We took (a, an) elevator to the main floor.

4. We had (a, an) up-to-date listing of exhibits.

5. There was (a, an) exhibit about the ocean floor.

6. It was (a, an) day to remember!

B. Write a noun on each line to complete the sentences.

1. We read a _____ about a _____.

2. The _____ in a funny story had an _____ for a pet.

3. We went to the _____ to get an _____.

4. Angela saw a _____ on the _____.

5. A _____ was curled up on the _____.

C. Complete the sentence with three singular nouns. Use the article *a* or *an*.

Molly drew a picture of _____

_____

Name

ARTICLES AND OTHER ADJECTIVES

A. Fill in the bubble next to the article that correctly completes the sentence.

1. I want to be _____ firefighter in our class play.
- ⬭ the
- ⬭ an

2. My friend plans to play one of _____ astronauts.
- ⬭ an
- ⬭ the

3. Sue read an exciting story about _____ acrobat.
- ⬭ an
- ⬭ a

4. We wrote letters to _____ authors of the book.
- ⬭ a
- ⬭ the

5. _____ illustrations were done in bright colors.
- ⬭ The
- ⬭ An

B. Fill in the bubble next to the word that best completes the sentence.

1. A few days ago, we went on an _____ ride!
- ⬭ train
- ⬭ elephant
- ⬭ boat

2. John visited an _____ outside the city.
- ⬭ airport
- ⬭ zoo
- ⬭ museum

3. Bill and Michelle shared an _____.
- ⬭ seat
- ⬭ umbrella
- ⬭ peach

4. At the edge of the water, Keesha saw a _____.
- ⬭ oyster
- ⬭ eel
- ⬭ crab

5. Rachel drew pictures of a _____.
- ⬭ octopus
- ⬭ lobster
- ⬭ egg

POSSESSIVE NOUNS

A. Underline the possessive noun in each sentence.

1. The king's palace is beautiful.

2. The palace's garden has many flowers.

3. The flowers' sweet smell fills the air.

4. The trees' branches shade the garden paths.

5. The gardener's tools are well-oiled and sharp.

6. People listen to the birds' songs.

7. The singers' voices are very beautiful.

8. The diamond reflects the sun's rays.

9. The diamond's light fills the palace.

10. Visitors' eyes open wide when they see all the colors.

B. Write each singular possessive noun from Part A.

1. _____   2. _____   3. _____

4. _____   5. _____

C. Write each plural possessive noun from Part A.

1. _____   2. _____   3. _____

4. _____   5. _____

POSSESSIVE NOUNS

> A **possessive noun** shows ownership. Add **'s** to make a singular noun show ownership. Add an apostrophe (**'**) after the **s** of a plural noun to show ownership.

A. Underline the possessive noun in each sentence. Write *S* on the line if the possessive noun is singular. Write *P* if the possessive noun is plural.

1. Anna's family took a walk in the woods. _____

2. They saw two birds' nests high up in a tree. _____

3. A yellow butterfly landed on Brad's backpack. _____

4. Anna liked the pattern of the butterfly's wings. _____

5. A turtle's shell had many spots. _____

6. Anna took pictures of two chipmunks' homes. _____

7. The animals' tails had dark stripes. _____

B. Complete each sentence with the singular possessive form of the noun in ( ).

1. Jim was going to play basketball at _____ house. (Carol)

2. One of _____ new sneakers was missing. (Jim)

3. He looked under his _____ desk. (sister)

4. He crawled under his _____ bed to look. (brother)

5. It was outside in his _____ flower garden. (dad)

6. The _____ lace had been chewed. (sneaker)

7. Jim saw his _____ footprints in the dirt. (dog)

POSSESSIVE NOUNS

A. Choose the singular possessive noun to complete each sentence.

1. Joan _____ backpack was stuffed with library books.
   - ◯ Kramer
   - ◯ Kramers'
   - ◯ Kramer's

2. She should have borrowed her _____ large book bag.
   - ◯ mothers'
   - ◯ mother's
   - ◯ mothers

3. Her little _____ book was due back by five o'clock.
   - ◯ brother's
   - ◯ brothers'
   - ◯ brothers

4. A sign on a _____ desk warned of fines for late books.
   - ◯ librarians'
   - ◯ librarians
   - ◯ librarian's

5. _____ heart raced as she got there just in time.
   - ◯ Joan's
   - ◯ Joan
   - ◯ Joans'

B. Choose the plural possessive noun to complete each sentence.

1. All the _____ telescopes were loaded onto the space shuttle.
   - ◯ astronomers'
   - ◯ astronomers
   - ◯ astronomer's

2. At take-off both _____ trails were long and straight.
   - ◯ engine's
   - ◯ engines'
   - ◯ engines

3. The _____ loud cheers filled the air.
   - ◯ spectators
   - ◯ spectator's
   - ◯ spectators'

4. Everyone applauded for the many _____ good work.
   - ◯ scientists'
   - ◯ scientist's
   - ◯ scientists

5. The four _____ pictures appeared on the news.
   - ◯ astronauts
   - ◯ astronaut's
   - ◯ astronauts'

SUBJECT AND OBJECT PRONOUNS

> A **pronoun** takes the place of a noun or nouns in a sentence. The words *I, you, she, he, it, we,* and *they* are subject pronouns. Use one of these pronouns to take the place of a subject in a sentence.

A. Underline the subject pronoun in each sentence.

1. We are going to the dentist.

2. It won't take long.

3. I went in first.

4. She asked the assistant for help.

5. He gave the dentist some pink toothpaste.

6. They said the toothpaste would taste like strawberries.

7. You will like the taste, too.

B. Decide which pronoun in the box can replace the underlined subject. Write the pronoun on the line. Remember to capitalize.

she	he	it	we	they

1. Dr. De Soto is a popular dentist. _____

2. Mrs. De Soto is his assistant. _____

3. The fox and the rabbit are waiting to be seen. _____

4. The fox has a bad toothache. _____

5. The chair is ready for the next patient. _____

6. Dr. and Mrs. De Soto do not trust the fox. _____

7. Roger and I enjoy reading this story. _____

SUBJECT AND OBJECT PRONOUNS

> A **pronoun** takes the place of a noun or nouns in a sentence. The words *me, you, him, her, it, us,* and *them* are object pronouns. Use these object pronouns in the predicates of sentences.

A. Underline the object pronoun in each sentence.

1. Aunt Cindy gave us a football.

2. Our dog Rex found it.

3. He thinks the ball is for him.

4. I said, "Rex, that's not for you!"

5. Aunt Cindy gave me another ball for Rex.

6. Now Rex always wants to play with her.

7. I like to watch them.

B. Decide which object pronoun below can replace the underlined word or words. Write the object pronoun on the line.

1. I went to the movies with Rachel and Kevin. _____

2. Kevin asked Rachel for some popcorn. _____

3. Rachel was happy to share the popcorn. _____

4. I accidentally bumped Kevin. _____

5. The popcorn spilled all over Rachel, Kevin, and me. _____

C. Write two sentences. In one sentence use a subject pronoun. In the other sentence use an object pronoun.

1. _____

2. _____

SUBJECT AND OBJECT PRONOUNS

Decide which pronoun can replace the underlined words.
Fill in the bubble next to the correct answer.

1. Uncle Sean is taking Melina and me ice skating at the pond.
   - ○ they
   - ○ us
   - ○ her

2. The pond freezes by late December.
   - ○ He
   - ○ You
   - ○ It

3. Melina knows how to skate.
   - ○ She
   - ○ Her
   - ○ I

4. Uncle Sean shows Melina how to skate backwards.
   - ○ her
   - ○ she
   - ○ them

5. I spot skaters nearby.
   - ○ us
   - ○ we
   - ○ them

6. Pablo and Kim are my friends.
   - ○ Us
   - ○ They
   - ○ Them

7. Uncle Sean skates over to say hello.
   - ○ It
   - ○ He
   - ○ Us

8. Pablo, Kim, and I listen to Uncle Sean's jokes.
   - ○ We
   - ○ Them
   - ○ Us

9. Everyone likes Uncle Sean.
   - ○ me
   - ○ he
   - ○ him

10. They will join Uncle Sean, Melina, and me for hot apple cider.
    - ○ it
    - ○ we
    - ○ us

POSSESSIVE PRONOUNS

A. Circle the subject pronoun in each sentence. Then underline the possessive pronoun. Use these answers to fill in the chart.

> **A possessive pronoun** shows ownership or belonging. It takes the place of a noun that shows ownership. *My, your, his, her, its, our,* and *their* are possessive pronouns.

1. I am planning a trip with my family.

2. Will you wear your sunglasses?

3. He will bring his camera.

4. She will take her dog along.

5. It will eat all its food.

6. We will enjoy our vacation.

7. They will show their pictures.

Subject Pronouns	Possessive Pronouns
I	my

B. Underline the possessive pronoun in each sentence.

1. The desert is their home.

2. Her umbrella blocks out the sun.

3. That javelina likes to play his guitar.

4. His address is 1 Tumbleweed Avenue.

5. Coyote said, "My stomach is growling."

6. "I'll blow your house down," Coyote shouted.

7. Its walls are made of tumbleweeds.

8. "Our house is strong," the third Javelina said.

POSSESSIVE PRONOUNS

Possessive pronouns show ownership or belonging. They take the place of nouns that show ownership. *My, your, his, her, its, our,* and *their* are possessive pronouns.

A. Complete each sentence. Write the correct pronoun in ( ) on the line.

1. Nicole likes to pick apples at _____ farm.
   (we, our)

2. Autumn is _____ favorite season. (her, she)

3. Dad says, "Please use _____ special basket." (I, my)

4. It was _____ birthday present from Grandpa. (he, his)

5. Dad said that _____ handle was carved by a famous artist. (their, its)

6. I tell Dad, "We will not forget to take _____ basket." (your, you)

7. Later, my mom and dad enjoyed _____ apple pie. (their, they)

B. Read each sentence. Write the possessive pronoun that can replace the underlined word or words.

1. The art project was due soon, but Zach's computer was broken. _____

2. My brother was using my family's computer. _____

3. Zach borrowed Angela's computer instead. _____

4. He loaded a picture into the computer's scanner. _____

5. Zach's idea was to stretch the picture into a funny shape. _____

6. Tim's and Ming's projects were exactly the same! _____

C. Write a sentence using the possessive pronouns *my* and *her*.

_____

_____

Name

POSSESSIVE PRONOUNS

A. Read each sentence. Fill in the bubble next to the possessive pronoun.

1. She is fixing her tree fort.
   - ○ She
   - ○ is
   - ○ her

2. Its roof started leaking after a storm.
   - ○ Its
   - ○ a
   - ○ after

3. Now we can eat our lunch without getting wet.
   - ○ we
   - ○ our
   - ○ without

4. I will share my favorite snack with a friend.
   - ○ I
   - ○ my
   - ○ will

5. He will bring his CD player.
   - ○ his
   - ○ He
   - ○ will

B. Choose the possessive pronoun that can replace the underlined word or words.

1. Erika's tire-patch kit is very helpful.
   - ○ My
   - ○ Our
   - ○ Her

2. She will use it to fix Brad's flat tire.
   - ○ he
   - ○ his
   - ○ their

3. The tire's inner tube has a slow leak.
   - ○ Its
   - ○ Our
   - ○ Their

4. Joel's and Diane's bike chains need to be oiled.
   - ○ Our
   - ○ Their
   - ○ Her

5. Now everyone can bike to my family's picnic.
   - ○ its
   - ○ our
   - ○ your

Name

COMPOUND SUBJECTS AND PREDICATES

A **compound subject** is two or more nouns connected by *and*. A **compound predicate** is two or more verbs connected by *and*.

A. Underline the nouns that form each compound subject. Then circle the word that connects the nouns.

1. Laura and Ramona are popular story characters.

2. In one story, Pa, Ma, and Laura traveled far.

3. The dog and horses trotted along.

4. Ma and Pa drove the wagon all day.

5. Grass and trees grow on the prairie.

B. Underline the verbs that form each compound predicate. Then circle the word that connects the verbs.

1. The wagon swayed and creaked.

2. Laura hummed and sang.

3. The road twisted and turned.

4. Pet and Patty neighed and snorted.

5. The deer stopped and stared.

C. Complete sentence 1 with two nouns joined by *and*. Complete sentence 2 with two verbs joined by *and*.

1. The _____ sang all day.

2. The dog _____ all the way home.

52 *Scholastic Success With Grammar • Grade 3*

COMPOUND SUBJECTS AND PREDICATES

A **compound subject** is two or more nouns connected by *and*. A **compound predicate** is two or more verbs connected by *and*.

A. Underline the compound subject or the compound predicate in each sentence. Write *CS* above each compound subject and *CP* above each compound predicate.

1. Mike and Jody moved away.

2. They often call and e-mail us.

3. Mike jogs and swims every day.

4. Phil and Jan will visit them.

5. Juan and Yoshi moved here from other countries.

6. They speak and read English very well.

7. Lori, Sam, and Beth wrote a play about moving.

8. They practiced and presented it to the class.

9. We clapped and smiled at the end.

10. The parents and the principal liked the play.

B. Complete one sentence with the compound subject. Complete the other sentence with the compound predicate.

My dad and sister   **barked and jumped**

1. Buster _____ when we got home.

2. _____ played word games for an hour.

COMPOUND SUBJECTS AND PREDICATES

A. Look at the underlined part of each sentence. Fill in the bubble that tells if it is a compound subject or a compound predicate.

1. My brother and I went to the grocery store in town.
   - ⬭ compound subject
   - ⬭ compound predicate

2. We talked and laughed all the way there.
   - ⬭ compound subject
   - ⬭ compound predicate

3. My sister and Mom met us at the store.
   - ⬭ compound subject
   - ⬭ compound predicate

4. We cooked and ate some delicious blueberry pancakes.
   - ⬭ compound subject
   - ⬭ compound predicate

5. The bus and train arrived late in the station.
   - ⬭ compound subject
   - ⬭ compound predicate

B. Complete each sentence. Fill in the bubble next to the compound subject or compound predicate.

1. _____ planned the class trip.
   - ⬭ Paul, Luz, and Annie
   - ⬭ The family
   - ⬭ The children

2. The _____ painted pictures of bears.
   - ⬭ I
   - ⬭ teacher and students
   - ⬭ We all

3. Jane _____ her poem.
   - ⬭ read
   - ⬭ wrote and proofread
   - ⬭ practiced

4. Dad _____ the letter.
   - ⬭ copied
   - ⬭ e-mailed
   - ⬭ stamped and mailed

5. My little brother _____.
   - ⬭ slept
   - ⬭ ran, skipped, and jumped
   - ⬭ woke up

CONTRACTIONS

A. Underline the contraction in each sentence. Circle the apostrophe. Then write the contraction on the line.

1. It's time for another adventure.　　　　_____

2. We're studying animal habitats.　　　　_____

3. They've made a habitat for Bella.　　　　_____

4. I'm sure that Bella is gone.　　　　_____

5. Wanda thinks that she'll be back.　　　　_____

6. They're in favor of going to find Bella.　　_____

B. Circle the contraction. Then, write the two words that make up the contraction.

1. I've gone on this bus before.　　　　_____

2. What's the bus doing?　　　　_____

3. It's shrinking to the size of a bullfrog.　　_____

4. The students say they're having fun.　　_____

5. "I'm hanging on for dear life," Liz said.　　_____

C. Put the two words together to form a contraction.

1. he + will = _____   4. I + am = _____

2. they + are = _____   5. we + will = _____

3. who + is = _____   6. there + is = _____

APOSTROPHE/CONTRACTIONS

Complete each sentence with a contraction
made from the two words in parentheses.
Write the contraction on the line.

> A **contraction** is a shortened
> form of two words.
> An **apostrophe** replaces the
> missing letter or letters.

1. _____ in the package? (What is)

2. My mom says _____ for me. (it is)

3. _____ so excited! (I am)

4. _____ birthdays great? (Are not)

5. I _____ wait to open my gifts. (cannot)

6. I hope my mom _____ mind if I tear the wrapping
   paper. (does not)

7. "Be careful. _____ very delicate," she says. (They are)

8. I _____ want to wait another second. (did not)

9. In fact, _____ never been very patient. (I have)

10. I _____ mean to keep you wondering. (do not)

11. In the box, _____ a tiny cat family made of china.
    (there is)

**Imagine not using any contractions when you talk. How long
do you think you could keep it up? Write what you think.**

CONTRACTIONS

A. Fill in the bubble next to the two words that make up the underlined contraction.

1. We're going to see a nature movie.
   - ◯ We have
   - ◯ We is
   - ◯ We are

2. "You'll learn about living things," our teacher said.
   - ◯ You are
   - ◯ You will
   - ◯ I will

3. We've been studying animal habitats in science.
   - ◯ We have
   - ◯ We are
   - ◯ You are

4. I'm writing a report on how animals communicate.
   - ◯ I have
   - ◯ I am
   - ◯ I will

5. It's about how animals use their senses.
   - ◯ It is
   - ◯ Is not
   - ◯ He is

B. Fill in the bubble next to the contraction for the underlined words.

1. The teacher asked, "Who is writing about birds?"
   - ◯ Won't
   - ◯ Who's
   - ◯ What's

2. There is a new bird exhibit at the museum.
   - ◯ There's
   - ◯ They've
   - ◯ Where's

3. I hope she will be there Saturday morning.
   - ◯ she's
   - ◯ I'll
   - ◯ she'll

4. The museum does not open until 10 A.M.
   - ◯ doesn't
   - ◯ didn't
   - ◯ isn't

5. Do not forget your notebook and pencil.
   - ◯ Doesn't
   - ◯ Don't
   - ◯ Shouldn't

USING PUNCTUATION

> **Quotation marks** show the exact words of a speaker. **Commas** appear between the day and year in a date, between the city and state in a location, and between the lines of an address.

A. Add quotation marks to show the speaker's exact words.

1. I have a strange case,   said Mr. Brown.

2. What's strange about it?   asked Encyclopedia.

3. Seventeen years ago Mr. Hunt found an elephant,   began Mr. Brown.

4. Where did he find it?   asked Mrs. Brown.

5. The elephant just appeared in his window,   answered Mr. Brown.

6. He must have fainted!   exclaimed Encyclopedia.

7. No, Mr. Hunt bought him,   said Mr. Brown.

B. Add commas wherever they are needed.

1. I go to the library in Huntsville Alabama.

2. It is located at 12 Oak Street Huntsville Alabama 36554.

3. The last time I was there was January 8 2001.

4. The books I checked out were due January 22 2001.

5. My cousin Jeb goes to the branch library at 75 Peachtree Lane Farley Alabama 35802.

6. Is it true that Donald Sobol once spoke at the library in Redstone Park Alabama?

7. He spoke there on September 29 2000.

8. He will soon read at 47 Draper Road Newportville Pennsylvania.

USING PUNCTUATION

> **Quotation marks** show the exact words of a speaker.
> **Commas** appear between the day and year in a date, between the city and state in a location, between the lines of an address, and after all but the last item in a series.
> **Underlining** shows book titles.

A. Read each sentence. Add any missing commas.

1. Mrs. Wu's bank is located at 92 Maple Avenue Inwood Texas 75209.

2. She opened an account there on September 8 2001.

3. She also uses the branch office in Lakewood Texas.

4. That branch is open weekdays Saturdays and some evenings.

5. The main office is closed Saturdays Sundays and all holidays.

6. Mrs. Wu saw Ms. Ames Mr. Pacheco and Mrs. Jefferson at the bank on Saturday.

7. They carried checks bills and deposits.

8. Mr. Pacheco has had an account at that bank since May 2 1974.

B. Read the sentences below. Add any missing quotation marks, commas, or underlining.

1. My favorite author is Jerry Spinelli   said Rick.

2. Spinelli was born on February 1 1941.

3. His home town is Norristown Pennsylvania.

4. What are your favorite books by him? asked Teresa.

5. I like Maniac Magee Dump Days and Fourth Grade Rats   replied Rick.

Write a sentence that tells your own mailing address. Then name three things you enjoy receiving in the mail, such as letters from friends, magazines, or catalogs.

USING PUNCTUATION

A. Each sentence is missing one type of punctuation: quotation marks, commas, or underlining. Fill in the bubble next to the type of punctuation that needs to be added to the sentence to make it correct.

1. We read a book called At the Zoo.
   - ⬭ quotation mark
   - ⬭ commas
   - ⬭ underlining

2. It had pictures of a lion monkeys and bears.
   - ⬭ quotation mark
   - ⬭ commas
   - ⬭ underlining

3. "Can we go to the wild animal show? asked Brent.
   - ⬭ quotation mark
   - ⬭ comma
   - ⬭ underlining

4. The show will be in town on June 8 2002.
   - ⬭ quotation mark
   - ⬭ comma
   - ⬭ underlining

B. Look at the underlined part of each sentence. Fill in the bubble that shows the correct answer.

1. I have a new baby sister! shouted Liz.
   - ⬭ "I have a new baby sister"!
   - ⬭ "I have a new baby sister!"
   - ⬭ correct as is

2. She was born on April 3 2002.
   - ⬭ April 3, 2002
   - ⬭ April, 3 2002
   - ⬭ correct as is

3. She was born at 1800 River Road, Centerville, North Carolina.
   - ⬭ 1800 River Road Centerville, North Carolina
   - ⬭ 1800 River Road Centerville North Carolina
   - ⬭ correct as is

4. She has tiny fingers tiny toes and a big scream
   - ⬭ tiny fingers, tiny toes and a big scream.
   - ⬭ tiny fingers, tiny toes, and a big scream
   - ⬭ correct as is

IRREGULAR VERBS

A. **In each sentence, underline the past tense of the verb in ( ). Then, write the past-tense verb on the line.**

1. Jessi told Jackie to be ready early. (tell) _____

2. He was nervous about his science fair project. (is) _____

3. Jackie's friends came to the table. (come) _____

4. They saw the volcano there. (see) _____

5. Jackie knew his speech by heart. (know) _____

6. The sign on the exhibit fell over. (fall) _____

7. The teacher lit the match for Jackie. (light) _____

8. Jackie threw his hands into the air. (throw) _____

B. **Complete each sentence. Write the correct verb on the line.**

fell   threw   saw   knew

1. Jackie _____ all about volcanoes.

2. He once _____ a real volcano.

3. It _____ ashes and fire into the air.

4. The ashes _____ all over the ground.

C. **Complete each sentence. Use the past form of *know* in one and the past form of *tell* in the other.**

1. When I was five, I _____

2. My brother _____

Name

IRREGULAR VERBS

Irregular verbs do not form the past tense by adding *-ed*. They change their form.

A. Complete each sentence. Write the past form of the verb in ( ).

1. Erin _____ dry lima beans at the store. (buy)

2. Her family _____ lima beans for dinner. (eat)

3. Erin _____ six lima bean plants for the science fair. (grow)

4. She _____ her project on Saturday. (begin)

5. Erin _____ three plants water and light. (give)

6. The other plants _____ all day in a dark closet. (sit)

B. Circle the past-tense form of the verb in ( ) to complete each sentence.

1. The judges (come, came) to Erin's table.

2. She (won, win) a blue ribbon.

3. Erin's family (went, go) to the fair.

4. One lima bean plant (is, was) 6 inches tall.

5. Two plants (fall, fell) over in the pot.

6. Erin (said, say), "I learned a lot."

C. Write a sentence about growing something. Use a past-tense irregular verb in your sentence.

_____

_____

62 *Scholastic Success With Grammar • Grade 3*

Copyright © Scholastic Inc.

Page 4
A. 1. Q 3. S 5. Q 7. S
2. S 4. Q 6. S 8. Q
B. 1. How did the ant carry the crumb?
2. She carried it herself.

Page 5
A. 1. Can we take a taxi downtown?
2. Where does the bus go?
3. The people on the bus waved to us.
4. We got on the elevator.
5. Should I push the elevator button?
B. 1. answers will vary
2. answers will vary

Page 6
1. correct as is 6. The man
2. help. 7. correct as is
3. would not help 8. from the ant.
4. the Ants 9. strongest.
5. cousins. 10. Do you

Page 7
A. 1. E 3. C 5. E 7. E
2. C 4. E 6. C 8. C
B. answers will vary

Page 8
A. 1. There's a Gila monster at the airport!
2. Look at the buffaloes.
3. Pack your toys and games.
B. 1. sentence
2. sentence
3. not a sentence; I want to be a subway driver.
4. sentence
5. not a sentence; I hope there are kids on our street.
6. sentence

Page 9
1. correct as is
2. excited!
3. pack.
4. adorable!
5. correct as is
6. Help me find a game.
7. correct as is
8. It will be great!
9. to write to me.
10. team won the game!

Page 10
A. 1. S 3. P 5. P
2. S 4. S
B. 1. sisters 4. parents
2. pockets 5. girls
3. fingers
C. Singular: train, cow
Plural: fences, gates

Page 11
A. ch, sh, ss, x: Possible answers: beach, fox, box, dress, boss, dish, fish
y: Possible answers: baby, bunny, city, berry, family, diary
f: Possible answers: calf, hoof, shelf, half, wolf
B. 1. cherries 4. boxes
2. bushes 5. shelves
3. peaches 6. classes
C. answers will vary

Page 12
1. boxes 6. brushes
2. teeth 7. groceries
3. correct as is 8. correct as is
4. glasses 9. mice
5. faxes 10. stories

Page 13
A. 1. common
2. common
3. proper
B. 1. April, brother, sister
2. Julius, May
3. Taiwan, parents
4. April, Saturday, school
5. Mandarin, language
6. May, Middle Ages, book
C. Common Nouns: camp, children, picnic
Proper Nouns: August, David, Fourth of July

Page 14
A. 1. Common: doctor; Proper: Pat
2. Common: park; Proper: Atlanta
3. Common: football; Proper: Tangram
B. answers will vary

Page 15
1. Fourth of July
2. correct as is
3. Tom's apple pie
4. teacher, Dr. Ruffin
5. correct as is
6. Kansas City, Missouri
7. New Year's Day
8. school on Monday
9. pets in North America
10. the movies on Saturday

Page 16
A. 1. S 3. P 5. S
2. S 4. P
B. 1. Singular: It
2. Singular: She
3. Plural: We
4. Plural: They
C. 1. he or she 3. they
2. it 4. she

Page 17
A. 1. us, P 4. it, S
2. him, S 5. me, S
3. her, S 6. them, P
B. 1. us 3. her 5. him
2. me 4. them
C. Sample answer: It is inside the house. I will get it.

Page 18
1. us 6. He
2. me 7. correct as is
3. correct as is 8. correct as is
4. It 9. It
5. them 10. I

Page 19
A. 1. cheered 4. serves
2. added 5. emptied
3. give
B. 1. paraded 4. skipped
2. whispered 5. bounced
3. gobbled
C. 1. laughed 3. whispered
2. sighed

Page 20
A. 1. snatched 3. nibbled
2. cracked 4. scrambled
B. 1. honked 4. ran
2. grabbed 5. bounced
3. shouted
C. answers will vary

Page 21
A. 1. arrived 4. ate
2. hugged 5. cheered
3. roasted
B. 1. chased 4. leaped
2. dashed 5. grabbed
3. peeked

Page 22
A. 1. past 6. past
2. past 7. present
3. present 8. present
4. past 9. present
5. past 10. past
B. 1. The man crossed the river.
2. He rows his boat.

Page 23
A. 1. fills 4. leave
2. watches 5. go
3. takes
B. 1. looked 3. walked
2. stared 4. helped
C. 1. Answers will vary

Page 24
1. correct as is
2. washes and peels
3. correct as is
4. enjoy
5. entered
6. traveled
7. arrived
8. awarded
9. correct as is
10. enjoyed

Page 25
A. 1. was 4. am
2. is 5. were
3. are
B. 1. past 4. past
2. present 5. present
3. present
C. 1. am 2. are 3. is

Page 26
A. 1. is, being
2. carried, action
3. were, being
4. are, being
B. 1. am 4. is
2. are 5. were
3. was
C. answers will vary

Page 27
1. are 6. was
2. correct as is 7. were
3. correct as is 8. were
4. were 9. correct as is
5. am 10. am

Page 28
A. 1. M 4. M 7. H
2. H 5. H 8. M
3. H 6. M
B. 1. will watch
2. is going
3. are reading
4. have lifted
5. had climbed

Page 29
A. 1. had built 4. will fly
2. has painted 5. will bring
3. is building 6. am buying
B. 1. is 4. using
2. had 5. will
3. going 6. have
C. answers will vary

Page 30
A. 1. reading 4. come
2. playing 5. share
3. walked
B. 1. has 4. will
2. is 5. have
3. will

Page 31
A. 1. is 4. were
2. am 5. are
3. was 6. will be
B. 1. am, present 4. were, past
2. was, past 5. is, present
3. are, present
C. 1. am
2. was
3. are

Page 32
A. 1. S 4. P
2. S 5. S
3. P
B. 1. was 4. is
2. were 5. are
3. am
C. answers will vary

Page 33
A. 1. is 4. were
2. am 5. was
3. are
B. 1. is 4. were
2. was 5. will be
3. are

Page 34
A. 1. All of the families (traveled to California.
2. Baby Betsy, Billy, Joe, and Ted (stayed in the cabin.
3. My father (told us stories.
4. I (baked a pie.
B. 1. Betsy 4. feet
2. miners 5. man
3. baby
C. 1. made 4. bakes
2. rolled 5. loves
3. added

Page 35
A. 1. class | took
Simple subject: class; Simple predicate: took
2. paintings | hung
Simple subject: paintings; Simple predicate: hung
3. Maria | saw
Simple subject: Maria; Simple predicate: saw
4. children | looked
Simple subject: children; Simple predicate: looked
5. Paul | pointed
Simple subject: Paul; Simple predicate: pointed
6. friend | liked
Simple subject: friend; Simple predicate: liked
7. Everyone | laughed
Simple subject: Everyone; Simple predicate: laughed
8. people | visited
Simple subject: people; Simple predicate: visited
9. bus | took
Simple subject: bus; Simple predicate: took
B. answers will vary

Page 36
A. 1. complete subject
2. complete predicate
3. complete subject
4. complete predicate
5. complete subject
B. 1. simple predicate
2. simple subject
3. simple subject
4. simple subject
5. simple predicate

Page 37
A. 1. big, sweet
2. many, hot
3. red, four
4. ripe, juicy
5. large, round
6. delicious, colorful
B. answers will vary
C. answers will vary

Page 38
A. 1. sparkling   4. Busy
2. clear   5. fresh
3. Large
B. Answers may include:
1. red   4. loud
2. green   5. sour
3. sweet

Page 39
A. 1. Several   4. blue
2. six   5. colorful
3. many
B. 1. delicious   4. five
2. many   5. wonderful
3. some

Page 40
A. 1. The, the   5. The, the, the
2. an   6. The, a
3. A, a, a   7. The, an, on
4. an   8. an, the
B. 1. a   4. an   6. the
2. the   5. an   7. a
3. the   5. an   8. a

Page 41
A. 1. an   3. an   5. an
2. a   4. an   6. a
B. answers will vary
C. answers will vary

Page 42
A. 1. the   4. the
2. the   5. The
3. an
B. 1. elephant   4. crab
2. airport   5. lobster
3. umbrella

Page 43
A. 1. King's
2. palace's
3. flower's
4. trees'
5. gardner's
6. birds'
7. singers'
8. sun's
9. diamond's
10. Visitors'
B. 1. king's   4. sun's
2. palace's   5. diamond's
3. gardener's
C. 1. flowers'   4. singers'
2. trees'   5. Visitors'
3. birds'

Page 44
A. 1. Anna's, S
2. birds', P
3. Brad's, S
4. butterfly's, S
5. turtle's, S
6. chipmunks', P
7. animals', P
B. 1. Carol's   5. dad's
2. Jim's   6. sneaker's
3. sister's   7. dog's
4. brother's

Page 45
A. 1. Kramer's   4. librarian's
2. mother's   5. Joan's
3. brother's
B. 1. astronomers'
2. engines'
3. spectators'
4. scientists'
5. astronauts'

Page 46
A. 1. We   5. He
2. It   6. They
3. I   7. You
4. She
B. 1. He   5. It
2. She   6. They
3. They   7. We
4. He

Page 47
A. 1. us   5. me
2. it   6. her
3. him   7. them
4. you
B. 1. them   4. him
2. her   5. us
3. it
C. answers will vary

Page 48
1. us   5. them   9. him
2. It   6. They   10. us
3. She   7. He
4. her   8. We

Page 49
A. 1. I, my   5. It, its
2. you, your   6. We, our
3. He, his   7. They, their
4. She, her
B. 1. their   5. My
2. Her   6. Your
3. his   7. Its
4. His   8. Our

Page 50
A. 1. our   5. its
2. her   6. your
3. my   7. their
4. his
B. 1. his   4. its
2. our   5. His
3. her   6. Their
C. answers will vary

Page 51
A. 1. her   4. my
2. Its   5. his
3. our
B. 1. Her   4. Their
2. his   5. our
3. Its

Page 52
A. 1. Laura (and) Ramona
2. Pa, Ma, (and) Laura
3. dog (and) horses
4. Ma (and) Pa
5. Grass (and) trees
B. 1. swayed (and) creaked
2. hummed (and) sang
3. twisted (and) turned
4. neighed (and) snorted
5. stopped (and) stared
C. answers will vary

Page 53
A. 1. Mike and Jody, CS
2. call and e-mail, CP
3. jogs and swims, CP
4. Phil and Jan, CS
5. Juan and Yoshi, CS
6. speak and read, CP
7. Lori, Sam, and Beth, CS
8. practiced and presented, CP
9. clapped and smiled, CP
10. The parents and the
principal, CS
B. 1. barked and jumped
2. My dad and sister

Page 54
A. 1. compound subject
2. compound predicate
3. compound subject
4. compound predicate
5. compound subject
B. 1. Paul, Luz, and Annie
2. teacher and students
3. wrote and proofread
4. stamped and mailed
5. ran, skipped, and jumped

Page 55
A. 1. It's   4. I'm
2. We're   5. she'll
3. They've   6. They're
B. 1. I've   I have
2. What's   What is
3. It's   It is
4. they're   they are
5. I'm   I am
C. 1. he'll   4. I'm
2. they're   5. we'll
3. who's   6. there's

Page 56
1. What's   7. They're
2. it's   8. didn't
3. I'm   9. I've
4. Aren't   10. don't
5. can't   11. there's
6. doesn't

Page 57
A. 1. We are   4. I am
2. You will   5. It is
3. We have
B. 1. Who's   4. doesn't
2. There's   5. Don't
3. she'll

Page 58
A. 1. "I have a strange case,"
2. "What's strange about it?"
3. "Seventeen years ago Mr.
Hunt found an elephant,"
4. "Where did he find it?"
5. "The elephant just
appeared in his window,"
6. "He must have fainted!"
7. "No, Mr. Hunt brought
him,"
B. 1. Huntsville, Alabama
2. Street, Huntsville,
Alabama
3. January 8, 2001
4. January 22, 2001
5. Peachtree Lane, Farley,
Alabama
6. Redstone Park, Alabama
7. September 29, 2000
8. Draper Road,
Newportville,
Pennsylvania

Page 59
A. 1. Mrs. Wu's bank is located
at 92 Maple Avenue,
Inwood, Texas
2. September 8, 2001
3. Lakewood, Texas
4. weekdays, Saturdays, and
5. Saturdays, Sundays, and
6. Ms. Ames, Mr. Pacheco,
and Mrs. Jefferson
7. checks, bills, and deposits
8. May 2, 1974
B. 1. "My favorite author is
Jerry Spinelli," said Rick.
2. Spinelli was born on
Feburary 1, 1941.
3. His home town is
Norristown, Pennsylvania.
4. "What are your favorite
books by him?" asked
Teresa.
5. "I like Maniac Magee,
Dump Days, and Fourth
Grade Rats," replied Rick.

Page 60
A. 1. underlining
2. commas
3. quotation mark
4. comma
B. 1. "I have a new baby sister!"
2. April 3, 2002
3. correct as is
4. tiny fingers, tiny toes, and
a big scream

Page 61
A. 1. told   5. knew
2. was   6. fell
3. came   7. lit
4. saw   8. threw
B. 1. knew   3. threw
2. saw   4. fell
C. answers will vary

Page 62
A. 1. bought   4. began
2. ate   5. gave
3. grew   6. sat
B. 1. came   4. was
2. won   5. fell
3. went   6. said
C. answers will vary